From
Dark Horse
Road

Ellen McGinn

A blue lake book

blue lake books acknowledges the ongoing support of The Canada Council for the Arts.

Editors: Luanne Armstrong and Dorothy Woodend

Cover illustration: "Horse of a Different Colour", a monotype and iris print by Karen Munteran, Saturna Island, BC, www.gulfislands.com/galleryrosa
Cover design and inside layout by Linda Uyehara Hoffman
Set in Adobe Garamond in Quark XPress 4.1
Printed at Hignell Book Printing

Published in Canada by blue lake books
3476 Tupper Street
Vancouver, BC
V5Z 3B7
Telephone (604) 874-1167
Email: dorothy@axion.net

National Library of Canada Cataloguing in Publication Data
McGinn, Ellen
From Dark Horse Road

ISBN 0-9730831- 3-1

I. Title.

PS8575.G49F76   2002   C813'.6   C2002-910952-3
PR9199.4.M39F76   2002

The Canada Council | Le Conseil des Arts
for the Arts | du Canada

For
Barbara Tinglin
with love

Table of Contents

Raspberry Picking

Before the babies of summer were born
I picked raspberries along the wild river.
Nobody ever knew what hill or stone
it sprang from. Up north, they said,
under the reindeer moss.
So it came down wide in August after supper.
My father drove us there
in the yellow truck,
kicking up dust along a skinny dirt road
that ended suddenly
like a ride at the Ex. under the long sun.
He could name the edges of things
so that you could sleep among trees
and touch their leaves in the dark
the way you knew your dolls.
And the berries were so thick
we could not talk
because our mouths were full
and the river might be another country
on the other side
when I stood with my toes in the shallow sand
the bush at my back
the nameless place beginning
somewhere in the middle
where the river left no trace.

In A Flowery Mead

For the morning of the aftermath,
I would put animals in the grass
so that the careful girl might not be so afraid
there in the normal day,
in the blue bright spring;
the small animals always there
at the bottom of tapestries
with so much wrath and significance.

The girl stands still
in the middle of her backyard,
no fences
it is an air force base
no one put up a fence
there was the DEW* line
she thought it came and went in the morningtime
and liked the unstopped lawns;
the scorched marigolds crackling
around the house kept robbers away
but even bread and brown sugar
from her mother's transubstantive palm
could not save her
outside in the world that day.

I would include a small perfection
of flowers vigorous
above the death above the bones

---

* Defence Early Warning

and ashes as they are
at the bottom of tapestries
with the modest creeping animals
in the new thick grass where she stands
                        the bomb would drop
was about to drop

What is she to do with so much destruction
her mother her father how
can she tell them— this is the thing
that blows up God — what she learned
after recess what the teacher said
came next what she watches formless
rise to fill the whole slow sky
black as grass in the eye of the sun
straight in the eye at three
the end of the world will not hold
in her head in Edmonton.

If she stands in the centre
away from her house
her parents will not die.

Other things rise, her breath
in the Ukrainian church, close to them
on winter days, too cold for normal mass.

Her breath rises white as the stone columns
and the terrible bearded priest

who eats peacocks and golden birds
and white fudge with Christmas cherries in it
every day, he is the only one
who can stop the bomb he is
so terrible himself if he speaks
those words he speaks they will make a fence
and its stone leaves her breath going straight up.

Later she will find bees
to put into jam jars
stuffed with clover she will
pound holes in the lid
with a nail so that
they can breathe and lead
safe lives for a day
as this is the best she can do
on an air force base
when she is six in the aftermath.

Jonesboro Slaughter

If you go into the woods today
  you better go in disguise
  if you go into the woods today
  you better go in the skies
  if you go into the woods today
  you're in for a big surprise.
  Consider the ways

                        to grandpa's house
the cabinet containing bunsen burners, retorts
                        (sharp) (shooters)
blackened spoons for melting lead
skeletal systems lettered
in an ordered evolution of what's what
squirrels & birds (& little girls)
somewhere between the furniture
and that acre of wood bang on,
under glass the pickled fetus
in a dusty jar turning,
the speckled glimmer of a
boy's own world. Jammed in.
Specimens. What a wonder!
What a straight thin light
                        breaks
into that cluttered nomenclature
breaks

but it's not like that, babies here
are born, not like that, says
Debbie protective of her boy Christ-
mas & guns secure under the trees
big-haired Deb of the tiny toon town

Surprise the toll was not
sadly, allegedly the boys made off—
It's all there. Sadly,
with all of grandpa's blanks blanks blanks but
          simply really good caring
          kids who went into the woods
into the woods
in disguise the big blue sky no warning
the bell rang for fire — tolled
for some other   kind
natural forces
          today's the day
the teddy bears have their picnic.
Better off for them in a burning building
                         no chance
there of being   shot but in the
cool shade when it is always a relief
to run toward   the squirrels & birds
the little teddy bears wait
          no alarm
nothing to tell of the leafing danger.

Prayer Book Card

Here is the world turned upside down in half
a glass of wine, and a cat in the sun.
The wine white; the cat black.
Louis Armstrong across the lane and the young men
on their balconies
on a summer evening.
Bye bye bya seeya
crows, cars, the windowbox
dense, and fat flowers full of still colour.
Two black crows alight on black lines
between us. The lazy young men, and the warm
sun on my cheek fingers up and down like
whole round notes.
The upright flower of such is the cloak
of Jesus. Nothing shivers now in this light.
Nothing trembles.

Advice To A Virgin

When you look up and see the silhouette
of a man in your doorway, do not
advance. If there is a tree
behind him, blossoming all at once
with small white flowers

continue to sip tea
and if he says encounters like this
are a natural phenomenon
pay attention to the huge scarlet poppies
lapping up the light

and remember those movies
when you were ten
remember some poor innocent
deep in the jungle

What's that sound? Like rain. But it can't be!

that soft continuous slurring
in the background
that you decide to ignore.
Like rain.
It's caterpillars falling
that soft light sound
falling by the hundreds of thousands.
A natural phenomenon.

Look at him through the wings of a dragonfly. Take notes.
He will fragment into colours
like a church window.
Then the tree alone stands.
Then you advance.
That is the Annunciation.

The Bread Women

All the madonnas came from Bohemia,
they swam across inland seas
their carved hands curled around every wave,
the light wooden women came buoyantly
to the cities, making bread and children,
whose pleated eyes sought forfeited places
in the strange green land of the mothers
where once they were trees.

Once they were entire forests full of quiet snow
and animals whose warm breath piled up in prayer.

And all the madonnas that came from Bohemia
stitched rooms together, made nests, made holy
bread and tucked the animals into tablecloths;
the linen borders of their country reminiscent
of something pure that troubled no one.

Because they had been trees they were competent,
because they baked bread they were saints
serenity relentless on their gentle faces.

My lady fair from Bohemia who spreads her skirts
wide the white loaves of bread
warm against her thighs,
not stopping to notice what she gives,
this sainted dame gives everything away

except the one red rose in her garden
that stayed put.
She tries to pry the flower away,
her virginity no doubt, her virgin status
but it will not budge,
this one blooms to her horror it blooms
all day and night until she can stand
its sweet smell no more,
until her skirts swell
up
like bread and she can no longer
take tea but rises haplessly
through windows
taken into the greedy embrace of hinterlands
that claim her.

The White Land

After the night came the white land,
soft with thistle seed,
tapering narrow as saints' feet,
the sky folding above them
again and again;
adjacent waters sinking
all that came before.

There is a geography to measure.
The incandescent land
requires calipers, a piece of chalk
to mark systemic faults,
though there is a tacit sense
of innocence,
the air vibrant with insect wings,
a host of white butterflies
rising from the bleached stones.

His findings noted the passage of glaciers
especially evident in escarpments
still heard breaking off
like pieces of porcelain.
And she thought,
placing a dry stone on her tongue,
no one has come here since that day,
no one has come.

She sits,
white stones burning her bare legs,
heat issuing out of the dry earth
supplies her warmth.
She looks down

at the shadow cast by her own body,
dreaming, absorbed by the hot white land,
alone until her skin prickles
and her head lifts, startled
and it is his gaze
his eyes there
and she in his notation.

But there is time enough,
time for the half-formed smile of her delight,
before he puts away his notebook,
before she turns to find her hat,
and they leave the white land,
stopping only to take corn from a farmer's field,
disappearing among the dense blue-green leaves
down different rows.

Birdwatching for Corpses on the Beach One Fine Day

I saw an eagle first. "My, what a fine day for a drive!" So we stop the car,

go back.

There is an eagle on a rock. Sitting.
The white head, the huge black wings folded
at low tide.
So the car stops and we look behind.
There! Around the bend.
That's where I saw the eagle.
Can we drive backwards around the bend in the road
where the eagle sits on a rock?
Reason says no of course not we can't.
Once a direction forward is established
one cannot go back, particularly
around bends.
My mother-in-law does not modulate much
and her voice is as even as steven.
C. says, "Sure we can!" and I think if he hadn't...
And the echoes of reasonable women wanting to drive on
move ahead continue in the same direction drive me
around the bend so I say automatically
"Of course not", too,
in that same flat broken voice the eyes
looking ahead, unvarying.
It was supposed to be stoicism or something.
Endless progression of dull stretches miles of flat grey road
and you what?
You girded your loins with with with

girding steel you set your sights on the horizon
and never looked behind or right or
left, for sure not left.

Sinister eagles, on rock not moving at all,
but fixed as the strongest will fix on the hardest.
So that the car stops and we must return and say yes.
Because an eagle that motionless huge on our rocking sitting
is not an everyday sight. You don't just drive by.

Drive away drive back drive me
around the bend I am glad.
For in these goings lie partings, the beak of love,
but I am too dramatic in these things,
lie convention killing all life, well
not all, just you and me then, killing us
and all that lies between all that lies
in the killing eagle.

And at last we are back and the eagle is back.
There. Too. Still. Now.
Then when we stop and look and think about
our ominous crouch eagles
"Why?" we think on a day as fine as this
and we crowd and peer and then
there are are vultures. Oh ugly!
Aren't they ugly things red wattles and all!
They hunch, do they not?
Hunch those awful old things.

Over what though?
He gets out of the car, goes down to the beach. Looks.
He looks. (Because if you remember way back
when you knew anything at all
we vultures were hunched over lunch.)

It is so damn hard to see from a car
but I would say wouldn't you
that he stops on the brink and looks down
from the brink to the beach and he stops there.
Dear me! What does he see?
"Come look", he says to me, "you must see."
The surprise, the suspense, the mystery
come and look.
"A dead deer on the beach a buck see its horns."
Dead on the rocks. We stare at the deer.
Why is it here on such a fine day?
Even on such a fine day vultures will be vultures
and circle. Come away!
From the black flapping red-headed four-flying vultures

the eagle flew off from his rock.
This is where I am going.
To a party on the mountain.
A tea party for Kathi
Because she is going away. She is moving.
And they are both there.
There is Kathi all sharp edges and points
green eyes like the blades of the grass.

And he is there too. She is leaving.
This is her farewell tea. A separation
overlooking the Strait of Juan de Fuca.
You can see the Olympian range.
You can see that everyone has brought food.
The best is pink and red. A rich Bavarian cream.
A special dish in a glass bowl so that you can see through,
like a pink heart oozing blood but
I am being too dramatic. It's delicious
full of egg whites. Egg whites, and yellow roses,
the old-fashioned kind that smell like roses
and are regaining popularity
because they smell like roses again, in a vase beside the luscious pink thing
not blood, pureed raspberries.

You don't even need teeth to eat it.
You don't even need teeth on such a fine day
when there are old-fashioned roses that smell
like the real thing again. That smell.
Her cheekbones are sharp too, like the creases
on maps folded up the wrong way in the car dash.
She doesn't like to stop either.
But they sit side by side on the sofa one last time
and eat heartily.
Patting each other from time to time.

Blue Willow

In autumn the sea comes into the house
and it is no longer urgent
to fix cats, faucets, hair, flap A to slot B
or dinner.
Labels on sealed jars of jam
peel away
and no one knows anymore
what is preserved or pickled;
cakes fall in the middle
too moist to rise,
and the blue willow plate
in the kitchen window
cracks across the fleeing lovers.

They used to turn into birds
on my father's plate.
He told the story,
tracing their journey
across tiny painted bridges,
the wicked magician a brushstroke away.
My father's finger
touched them all;
how could they reach the sea
without him?
He said, "There is the boat."
"Where, where is the boat?"
the lovers asked.

Hidden, it was always
hidden beneath the blue willow boughs.
My father knew
they would be saved,
but I was never sure,
the magician crossed the water, too.

The little lovers embark
they do not know
how to become birds,
but they ascend anyway,
plump blue doves on my father's plate.

Autumn and the sea comes in
with stray cats and old songs.

The blue shag wall to wall
fluctuating like a pulse
beneath the surface,

and the room empty;
someone has left the radio on
duke duke duke duke of earl
on and on unraveling
through the house

The Little Girls Made Death

The little girls made Death and left him
in the front hall. The washer, the dryer,
and Death in the front hall. Stuck on the end
of a broomstick so we'd know he wasn't
just a doll, or the mop that made do
as a princess beside the well, and her long
hair. The door always open, Death there
sullen and green as apples that reek
of green things in other times – madness,
plague, the earth beneath wet stones.

The little girls left Death, carelessly
went away. The head a mask someone
must have worn once, worn him out
one windy night in winding sheets.
O pale and perilous Death in the hall!
The washing machine whiter than whites
your rage. For the little girls draped you
like a may-pole with their mother's scarves
but they did not stay to dance.

Drapery fine and fancy folds of silk swirl
round no sign of feet and Death's head
topped almost nothing but these frail folds
with patterns of flowers and green borders
foliage sprays of pansies or petunias or
blossoming boughs who can tell on silk

on water on death melting into a popsicle
purple and lime green, like a crayon

I once had for outlining the spots on clown's clothes.

The little girls said they would teach me to fly
before noon but they suck the honey
from purple clover and scream down the green grass.
They follow the deer into the woods.
Death's head glares at me but I can do nothing.
Except set the cycle for a cold wash
so that the colours hold fast.

The Chilling of the Dress

The dress keeps the vegetables cold
in folds like snow.
The dress, the dress is cold white breath
deep in the house, under the eaves,
down in the basement, permafrosting
all the lovely apples in heapy sleeps,
all the slouched potatoes up against the wall,
and onions in a fog because she
slipped out, a slip of a thing from some other plant
that didn't take in Rexdale.

Who'd take Rexdale?

She thought she could
for a day or two. It might be fun,
she thought, and looked up 'fun' in Webster's.
"It's goings-on," he said, "of a lively nature,"
but was not specific.

So she put away her wedding gown
and had five kids so fast that
she shut them all out of the house
and lit a cigarette.
They milled around the back door
angry as a bunch of bees, and their noses ran.
Then the tree in the front yard died.
God, what awful kids they were!

The lawn shrank, the diapers stank,
the children barked outside the door.
But the dress remained fresh
as stone and down she went to
the oh so cold room, the quiet
vegetables, gentle Jesus asleep in the hay,
and tried it all on again.

Then he was Rex,
sexy Rex dangling down in the dale.
How frail the lounging golden lawn
where they lay in concupiscent ceremony,
drinking each other, and now the dress
mad as a hatter in its Bay box.
"Webster," she whispered, "what have I done?
If I sing to the dress shall it dance?
If I cut up the dress with my red-handled
scissors, will it foam at the mouth and expire?
If I play an old tune to the violin dress
will the tree on the lawn leaf again?"

Above, the coiled house digests her,
each unhurried room
kept cool and dry, the grass brown.
The children at the door cry:
oh ghosts and goblins and witches!
oh snakes and snails and water buffaloes!
But they cannot scare her out.

Notions

More than the vampires
the gerbils upstairs
bothered Muriel.
Her neighbour fed
all the babies
to snakes, every one;
sold them to pet stores,
except for the batch
she put in the freezer
for another day.

The vampires ushered Muriel
along passages dangerous
for a woman alone.
Two gentlemen,
somewhat pale,
nails pared, in clean shirts;
they really were no bother.
"But the woman upstairs?"
Really a nice woman,
said the vampires,
believes in fresh air and exercise.
"But," said Muriel,
"she takes her lovers
into the bedroom,
while her husband
watches TV 'til 1 a.m.

and the gerbils are distraught!"

Nonsense. A clean house,
said the vampires,
well-behaved children.
"Even so," said Muriel
and thought, how damn conservative
these vampires are.
How little blood they take
from all my stories!

How They Appear

Once you start noticing leaves, they are everywhere.
But since it is winter, and so many people
have died, they are all of them on the ground
frosted flat, all
with arms spread out
as if they could embrace more leaves,
or still they were meant to be held to a tree.

Once you step out your door, they are down
everywhere, imprinted on the sidewalk
imprinted in frost, some bearing a resemblance
to skin, the ridges piling up
in a dune of slack leaves the way skin appears
beneath a microscope or as death
suddenly on one day, to many.

Astronomical Observations

There can be days   between the leaf and the distant stars,
descending   as there is darkness above
and below as above
as usual.
But how does the leaf fall   how does anything come down
from that spectral braille   scrawling a litany of galaxies,
white as the dandelions that used to measure floating worlds
being borne away?

Easy then to step   from the back porch into the sky,
the shadows beneath   and the green weeds
flourishing in shade, their bitter smell
and death passing   by painting lamb's blood   on every door
though I was safe in the month of May
mater oh mater   full of pulchritude and grace
and always ascending always world without end.
Up and away you went I thought you would never
disappear there was so much of you to go.

Too big for me the unbounded spaces   happening in silence without
edges.
I want the astonished man who saw   the other side of things
meeting the day, reasonably; the expected firmament
rustling with angels, and still he could see   his breath among them all
and looked beyond, the huge sky   creaking with the weight of stars
his hands spread like sails upon the night.

Brown Earthen Cups, On Clean Shelves, Over Sink

I did not use to stare at cups, like a sleep-walker.
Old bones have been found
in the sand of Ethiopia;
four million year old bones,
pre-dating the newer bones
of Lucy, our ancestor,
whose known bones, says the paper,
are earliest: a link so they think,
connecting us to apes.
I am on my hind legs staring at cups — it's quite a leap —
the creature (as they call our connection) lived in woodlands
and I remember the hands on cave walls in the spring
twenty thousand years ago.

A spider spins beneath the table, a good sign I'd say,
for the dog sleeps there, and I am somewhere
between in a woodland, beneath a tree uncertain
of where I was heading four million years ago;
knowing that I was no longer an ape, but
not knowing what, not knowing about Lucy,
or the blue hands, or the earthen cups in the cupboard.

So I sat there, still furry, beneath a tree. Evolving,
that's what I did that day, the sun still warm
on my fur. Looked up at the sun, sensed vaguely
it had been there before, with me
and that it had happened recently,

yesterday when I had been an ape, there was the sun,
and today anticipating Lucy I dreamt,
my eyes open I dreamt a tree,
then Lucy beneath, eyes wide, staring
into the darkness, and I was the darkness.

Intransit-ive

We have become more interesting
now that the kite will not ascend.
Is it any wonder that everyone
on the beach stops and watches
waiting for it to fly?
The children run to the sea the dogs
run after balls the waves roll
and crash and crash and crash
boom they go boom again
boom.

She says if she drives by herself
at a quarter to midnight she will die
on the road between Halifax
and the airport. A bad stretch in winter,
the lakes close over Christmas Eve,
below the ice her eyes silvering,
red berries in the tangled thicket
where birds fly in and out.

Waves crest white and break if she had sharp scissors
she could cut her way out of her family
snip snap she lies sleepless in their seamless flesh.

If she drives by night she will die;
they are all like that, so extreme,
so putting the tree in the front room

where no one sits.
She in the room at the end of the hall
drinking brandy reading Gone With the Wind
again, all the doors shut for winter
and no one comes down.

It's an empty moon on the road
she will not go up,
an empty place to come to, this room.
The guest waits at the airport and waits,
the clocks twist toward midnight,
all the lights spread an even blue
over the covered lakes.

.

A Baba Yaga Saga

Long ago before performance art
a woman went to Russia for a rest,
off she goes to Baba Yaga's house *
hippity hopping all about
the golden field,
that house could never settle down
a case of nerves amidst the alien corn.
"Relax!" yelled Baba Yaga, to her
hopping hut,
"roost awhile we have a guest."

She caught a carp and stuffed it
with ornamental eggs laid
by her hennicky hutch,
snapped off barley sugar fingers
for dessert, they grow back
pink and sticky, the eggs
hatch into houses gobbled
bones and all
          "Tell me, tell me!"
          croons Baba Yaga,
crunch cracking egg bones
with her five wooden teeth
talking with her mouth full of house,

"Do you come from a place
where two rivers converge

---

* Baba Yaga, a witch figuring in Russian fairy tales,
lived in a house on live chicken legs

32

where salmon spill and die
turn white and mountains
cloister cold as angels
in the snow?"

"That doesn't sound like Toronto,"
said the woman from elsewhere,
"Not the room where Great Gram Peters
    lived on dried fruit
    swore in Czech
    stayed in bed for days on end
    made me a doll
Mona black eyed Mona
of the black wool braids,
she leaked herself out
of her thin pink skin
soft wads of cotton batting,
Mona made of the dried fruit
body of my granny wrinkled sweet,

hated purely from her long years
hated purely in her Czech oaths,
she married a man with a mouth
like mine   clickity clack sang her beads
                in the back room,

peeled almonds, drank dark beer,
kept alive on wheels of honeyed quince,
ropes of figs hung from her ceiling;
one day she climbed up to heaven
left her teeth on a fat feather pillow
became a saint next to the knees of Jesus
a patron saint for those who hate well."

"Time to go!" screamed Baba Yaga,
"get outta here!", and she kicked
the restless woman out of her
chicken legged house.
"Come on back some day!"

Back where?

"Don't you come from a place
where the train whistle blows
out of town twice a day,
where your daddy hoes tomatoes
all in a row and you root heliotropically
in the ripe sun?"

"Once, in Fredericton …"
but the shack helter skeltered,
forsook the restive guest
somewhere near the gelid grey
Black Sea.

What the Butcher's Wife Knew in Toronto

[on the home front a fake:
a plastic image of the Sacred Heart,
the sacred —
a beat
in the boroughs]:

blood flowed and tears fell
from almost real eyes
an open and shut Jesus

sat in the middle of the floor
bled almost arterially
from a neon tube
that came out of his heart

sacred heart of Jesus
savior in the living room

when I was young
it replaced furniture
glowed at night
melded to the spot
he took a fit and bled to death—
heart-broke —
of the sacred   drip drip dripping
on the living room floor

below dark rooms
vinegar dark
and the elastic litany
of loose-fingered martyrs
wayward saints —
their lop-slided intercessions

Holy Mother carry me dear down
from this mountain weight
of bovine saints
down to the bottom
of the clip clop sea

take the scented wait of holy days
offerings of marbled meat
streaked white
with the fatted lamb of God
there in the middle bleeding
bleeding three fat drops

Sunday Papers

Anyone noticing the Greeks lately
sees the eye elliptical, fishy,
on those vases trace an ovoid geometry
that repeats and repeats. What
has that got to do with a Sunday morning quickie?
And afterwards. Cinnamon buns at Solly's.
    Shared Success at Van City
    Your Share Is Right
    right inside me
    apple closeouts
    who processes
    this digital hic-
    cupping body
Anyone with an eye like yours
can discriminate between mine
and a Greek vase. I am not
encircled by a tire tread motif
obligingly static forever
around our tableau.

How Anything Happens

I drink milk and you talk about chaos theory,
in profile. You look away.
What is it about chaos theory that you have to look away? Is it
on the other side of the room? It is not me.
I am a woman drinking milk sitting across from you at last.
There are patterns of chaos, I have seen pictures
and you agree that there are but any one
of the planets could fly out of its orbit
right now this very second, and my eye
brightens at the possibility because you are looking
straight at me in case planets plummet from their orbits
in a moment of abandoned chaos but I drink milk
carefully and imagine kissing your mouth
one of these days I shall do that. I have my finger prints
all over you, this predatory side of pouring milk.

A man averts his face, prefers to discuss chaos theory
when his father is dying upstairs,
or the woman across from him contemplates
his mouth as if they were already lovers,
and she is poised like an Egyptian cat lapping cream
as his profile explains what there is across the chaotic room
about to send a planet careening out of its normal milk run
and this perks her up. She knows which one.
Venus of the clouded atmosphere her hot surfaces
making everyone nervous. She is the one.
It's said to rain there every day. A wet place.

She is not surprised.

And when his father died she did not mourn, no
she did not. She pulled out maps and saw
there were places not mentioned in the cosmography
of chance, so was not surprised at the struggle to breathe
his last.
And didn't his own father come for him
out of the shadowed hallway
bulkier than all the silence
falling upon that house?
With the already dead, and the men
who argued chaos and stars from their orbits

and I dream of kissing you, though all this
is a matter of fact and to be expected:
the death, the kiss, the way of chaos.
Surely there is room to give way
to the rain falling on Venus
rendering all features indistinct save
those places where the eagle
hangs motionless over the Pass,
and wind quickens the marsh water,
and a blade of grass balances silver beads
as round as milk bubbles at the corner of my mouth.

Unscheduled Events

She falls   she falls and darkness enters,
surrounds her   not night on each side,
not the burning stars or the right moon
waxing high   but more and she — oh!
she says   oh and oh   she breathes
all dark cloudiness and disruption,
walks   along transformed faults, lines
of transgression   half drunk up roads
that cave in and water trembles
with every wayward breeze   Unconcerned,
the trees crack and fall   blessed coming down
blessed coming   back to a place, and easily
the wind across skin moves   in silver traces that appear
and move and disappear   fast these moments
sliding by the slippery heart like fish.

This is how it happens; first,
the roads erode on her   trees uproot, then
the earth collapses in a roar that was said
to sound like a train in the night,
a piece of Antarctica that breaks
into the opaque sea.

Examinations

I study rocks in my cubicle in the new library,
read of their fiery beginnings,
walk into the afternoon,
the row of rocks in order
alongside the ordered bed
a bed of groundcover.
Arranged stones, ground cultivated,
no resemblance to the diagrams
of intrusive felsic eruptions.

The long boulevard empty on Saturday afternoons
in the too bright spring.
Two crows in the top branches of an empty tree
do not necessarily mean anything
is about to happen
though I am glad to see them there,
their suspension in that tree
at that moment a pronouncement
from some other world that almost speaks.

I wait for the bus and sit on the grass welling up
in a smell I recognize as mine,
near me a young woman, two young men
she turns her head I hear her say words,
when I am married, she says, the bed
will be que sera sera sexy,
her face jumps out into the precise light,

lascivious, unmade.
Something leapt out, the bus pulls up,
not a cloud in the melliflous sky
not a single thing at all
just a silver plane glittering.
Off we go along the boulevard
past the bare and delicate trees all crowding together
all bending in the same direction.
We pass trees. I want to reach
for the next thing nothing is there;
to leap not knowing
not having to arrive in a known place
not knowing stones or crows or even trees,
not knowing the wanton girl the cloudless sky
but glad to have these
so that I may get from place to place
in all this emptiness.

Before Everest

High today hills and the houses on top:
neutrino stars, Everest and the price
of tea at The Peninsula,
"You must try it you must at least
once," she claps her hands,
little birds of paradise; some journeys
begin simply enough. In Hong Kong
hills snatch at the sky, not even trying to get away,
farther and farther from home
dense blue becoming a mountain
between pine trees.

I still have four cakes, and scone crumbs
on my pen; water whitens the sky,
wind blows, but the white sky will not move.
I can walk through doors now; it must be
those petit fours on my plate, gold-braided
doormen winking at me, the glass egress
benign as butter. Hot today the sun burns
through, orange, like a lit cigarette —
must be Buddha smoking up there, big and bronze
eyes closed on one of those mountain cones
bending over me. She never mentioned him

my travel agent with the tangerine finger tips on 4thAvenue,
or the stone lions I had to pass by to take tea
at the Peninsula. They are the doormen to the sky

the judges staring across the street
up at neutrino stars, at Everest in the distant middle,
at the hills above Hong Kong, Buddha's butt
squashed into the thick cotton sky. At 3 a.m.
I am glad to dream of water. I think we are ferrying
into the round mountain tops where Buddha smokes,
and angels throw petals down so that something
may cover my head before Everest.

My Sister's Kathmandu Period

She passes me her summer nightie white
and sudden as the wings of an owl I saw
opening like eyelids in the rearview mirror,
and my sister's eyes float huge and blue
behind her glasses. None of us can see.

I was on the road to the ferry at the end
of summer. No one else except the owl
behind me and the writing on the mirror
interpreting objects closer
than they might appear. Whoosh. Gone.

Rushing past she says, take care look after —
Gone. Up the stairs of her house
swept daily by the local help.
All night the wild dogs in the streets
yellow dogs worrying the moon;
then the cuckoo birds calm as fence posts
on and on until the kettle clatters, bangs
the streaky light into sense.

When I open my eyes the sky is the colour of violets.
Why does my sister cry in the time between
the wild dogs and the cuckoo
before tea and the light comes?
What radiant absence shines in the night?

lady bird lady bird fly away home your children
cannot comfort you their arms break off

The road dipped and rose again with an owl
in the back seat closer than it might appear
but I felt fine.

My pale pink sister breasts by me slow as a frieze;
at intervals her blood — three fat drops —
round as arms heavy as a low spring sky
falls onto the marble floor — cool in summer
cold in winter —
    (even her doll Sylvia was a platinum blonde,
    wore the best dress with lace and refused to share;
    we never played going to Kathmandu or children,
    the dolls enjoyed organized outings, long baths,
    sacrificial rituals,) dark red
and round round on the stairs.

An owl too close with the day
curved and downy
smells of church pews
unletters m-i-c-e
dry and precise
loamy in the back seat.

There is no yellow line
in the middle of the road
and the distant stars

anaemic now,
all the cedars stand.
The first fat drops of rain fall
and darken circles, drawn on pavement, porches,
unsheltered places
not knowing how to soak up
(the way blood falls on marble)
a body's blood,
no protection.

She flees past me pursued by her son.
How fleet she is in an emergency's
swift urgencies.
Her son in cape and sword
stands still, Super Daniel, he kills
monsters for her; lions erupt
from tended
turned up flower beds
with all bloody awful
bloodied jaws.

why is mummy bleeding?

yes sing the drops
blood drops, rain drops,
what else drops? snow drops?
rose red, the hunter —
the snow the woods,
woo woo the woods

My first morning I hear her crying.
I see her rich blood on the marble floor,
then another and another.
I follow her up the stairs,
cover her tracks with Kleenex
obliterate each and every round red drop.
She goes by a blur of whiteness and floating
eyes.

I saw an owl in the mirror
and Princess Diana died as the ferry left
Lyall Harbour. When I opened my eyes
the sky was the colour of violets.

My sister has a garden in Kathmandu

where a dry leaf spins around once,
a huge armored crab
in a square of concrete.
The wicker chairs are warriors
terrible on horseback,
disciplined, advancing,
in my sister's garden.
The bird-shit an elegant chalk white script
on the side of a mountain,
one word curved as a scimitar,
which the prophet himself daubed white
with chalk and shit, part of the
mountain lines
drawn.

And skin, my skin.
A thousand rough ridges, thickenings,
loosenings, bumps, and pitted places.

I should do something. Remove
the uneven blotches, wipe the slate
clean; the slack take up, take in,
the bumps and lumps and tag ends:
hormonal defects and lying sleepless
at night in Tibet putting you
together like a puzzle
night after night. I move

you around change how I lie in bed
to fit you. The shadows of clouds
olive on the dun skin
of the land, the minute changes
creeping across my skin. Why
can't I be milky meeting you now,
a promised land running with honey?

The Way An Egg Is A Gift

1.
    There was once a time
when I held
two eggs,
one in each hand;
my fingers curled
easily
holding the loose light
around an egg:

one to put into the sea
the other to eat with strawberries

Waiting for summer became me,
the way some women lean
into the gravid certainty of love,

their faces blunted
and simple
with the perfection
of the oracular:

an ordination
of bluebirds
spelt upon
the spirant sky

and I would lie

in the long grasses
as if waiting
grew in me
like rain.

2.   This is a fairy tale. Really
I went to Kathmandu; held
two eggs one in each hand
for the children's supper.
I was the visiting sister
and had come a long way.
The sea did not twist
in a slack skein
of jumbled shapelessness
as it might have;
we were land-locked
and your kitchen a quiet bureaucracy
of interiors.
It was the season for mangos
and fits of crows shook
into trees
stuttered with light
every evening.

Bestowing trust
like untroubled potentates
your children let me
arrange their bright
plastic place-mats

and balance two eggs
as they waited,
cupping me
in the ellipse
of their acceptance

then the water boiled
then the rooks cronked

and all the shadows
bundled in corners

you took the eggs
out of my hands
gently,
and you said, carefully,
reasonably,
eggs must never
ever ever
be put in water here
I've told you
the water here
I thought you knew
the water here is bad—
But boiled?
No! Never.

3.   So you see
this could not be a fairy tale.

I was sent out of my sister's kitchen
and put in another room.
She waited on me,
brought me white wine
and The Kathmandu Post.
I read about the increase
of snake bites
after the rains.

My Sister in Maitland, Nova Scotia

You were proud of your green apple tree
you said you pruned last year,
and now it bounds in leafy arcs
sprung loose from the knuckled core,
green apples studded into spiral
of incidental direction

like the drifting arms of undone galaxies,
you have always imagined these things.

The old rose bush cock-eyed
with coming back — you told me
how you sheared back
one hundred years of fisty tangle
into this swagger of white buds.

They were all there.

The old house plain and square
as the ship-builder's hands
that moored her to a lot
with knotted spruce and field stones
so she wouldn't slide out,
down the red mud banks of the Shubennecadie
and sail,
windows all ablaze with burning leaves, beyond.

So she wouldn't!
Reality gets us into such a state.

We sit on your back step
holding mugs of coffee.
Behind us in a field the sun
cannot get through the mist,
though it tries.
One green apple grasps
the sun bends around
in a quick curve,
holds us where we are,
the deft light stopped on a rim of skin

I know apples and peoples have to do with a geometry
of lines travelling in the most convenient direction
from a source across the road above a field

where a white mist rises and light
struggles out of this simplification:
the terror of so much distance.

I know it has to do with my father's hands
that will not reach for me
when I leave,

the way light touches
what is there and how what is there
waits. I remember

how once you held up half a lemon to explain
the sun's rays radiating so clear straight
from the obvious centre
in a lemon cut in half
its centre fixed
where a centre ought to be,
neither wandering nor about to leave,
this sun stayed put in your hand
where you could manifest the weight of light.

A Poem Interrupted

The cold white mist blows across her eyes
she cuts a persimmon in half
a silver spoon in her mouth
copper on her eyelids —
"Hey wait a minute!" said the woman
in the flowered hat. "I thought we
were in Tibet at an altitude of 5020 metres
sitting on yaks and—"

She picks her way down the stony slope
to a place where the land falls away
like the moon. And nothing moves.
"Somewhere below Everest, right?"
Nervously the woman took compass readings,
and an herbal tisane to remedy her shattered
categories. "Can't we keep this local?"

A place under a spell. No shore. No liminality
as far as the eye can see. She thinks, "I will
not find my home before night," and holds half
a persimmon in each hand, dense as bee's jelly.
"Uncanny," said the woman of flowers fanning
herself with The Lonely Planet, "I've often been
to parties with a similar minimal of liminals
and stringed quartets in the alcoves at Christmas.
Perhaps Prague or the Latent Hinterlands."

A girl who picked strawberries,
wore a wide brimmed hat
She could be a Botticelli
a Modigliani
a slice of lemon;
saints want to be her eyelids
sliding shut like Woolworth's lipsticks.

"If this riddlesome girl contrives to recur."
said the fat fretful flower frocked femme,
"we will certainly never arrive.
Tell her to quit this discursive fit.
I want to be in Tibet.
It's sad that she's stranded
in chilly white mists
location abstract and unnamed,
but I'll be in Lhasa late
while she deliberates
whether to be
or be not."

The Real Tibet

I try I do
but I know I'll fall in
if we stay at The Sno-Lion
where all the expeditions stay
with their crampons and tampons
and ice picks.

I cannot go out
in the alley at night
to pee as I must
at night as I do,
much as I want to stay at the place
where the expeditions begin I am not
brave enough to commence.

the dark alley, the cold — alright,
I did this in Middle Musquodobit
in the dead of winter, in love,
minus 25, crunching through blue snow,
myopic in moonlight,
the outhouse door frozen open
so I could look into the all holy night
and pee there reverently,
but this — !

dank shack, a plank with a hole
cut for my white western ass,

then nothing —
a dark shit pit,
I will topple
down where the wild dogs snuffle
happy as pigs in the proverbial,
I will fall
tangled in flannel,
the nightie I took for cold nights,
like this one,
where expeditions begin
below Everest.

I cannot stay, I'm sorry,
please send my regrets
to Sir Hilary and — and all the rest.
Tell them
in Middle Musquodobit when I was 25
I could pee in a blizzard,
the wind chill up my nightie,
the fearless stars roaring overhead.

Your silence is as big as Tibet where my sister sits beside a
stream dipping prayers

Finally, like a garden turned;
the end purple with holy days;
and silence:
the rushing away of something not there
maybe of water. I'll need a boat

to row through the silent day
to evening where the blue blue hyacinth
falls to its side facing west.
Today I burnt your downloaded
photo
beside the blue hyacinth;

is this an end of something, an end of you
without a word; the slow deeping upward
to stars, your face at last?

What was it after all but an accumulation
of bright dots digitalized.

Everything Is Different There

Where the tulips bend by weight
of their own red and cannot hold up
you know you have come
unprepared. Where is your sun hat?
You do not have the right currency.
Not for this country.

I should read the papers read about
floods happening everywhere, last night
I hear that red is picked out, seen, sorted;
a band in chaos. Abandoned
like tulips in clay pots
a chaotic red unable to hold up,
that edge to everybody wanting
to fall.

Sunday in Salisbury

This is a close
an end
a closed place
quiet walled
flowering chestnut trees
green wind
a confusion of birdsong.

Three little dogs
get their picture taken
beneath the chestnut tree.
A man
with silver hair
smiles at me
and the dogs,

passes by again.
I sit on the grass
he approacheth
he passeth by,
isn't it a lovely place,
he says. I agree.
How agreeable.

You restless
full of bus schedules
train schedules

where to go what to do.
You say today
you want to be
in motion.

I sit on the wide
closed grass.
Off you stride
twenty minutes away
a view, a picture
to take of doves
mournful mournful.

I'm drawn to stones
and still places,
wells water large trees.
You want to walk, fast.

(The flowering tree we are under
red red red)

Adrift

I have forgotten
in all this chaotic red
and gold between, forgotten everything
again; a space to fill, a place to be
and Mozart or somebody filling
the time so well; well bred
while the roses in the canal
float aloud aloud
and the bloated dead thing floats
with them, heavy not recognized
        a bird a rat a cat

We are walking along the canal,
red and pink roses, a champagne cork,
the dead thing, and an elephant
among the trees.
We must be near the London Zoo.

What of the gold between the trees and saints
and the trees themselves, skipping over stones,
and water and gold everywhere?
A man who says life has no meaning anymore.
This house cracks holding the two of us here.
My body inside far away recalls
the no place ever to be
the colour of thin gold
between trees and the saints once.

Far off once
I laid me down beneath you
beneath a tree
beneath the music
now I am no place
there are borders around

 *

I loop the loop of boundaries
and times and people I have seen enough
the king, the old stone, the Celtic cross
bright grass the violets there
blue fields but where am I
where are you?
Only vast goings vastly unmet
gone to dale and dell
too tight the world the order
of things the temperate climate.
I fight to breathe air and you.

Listen, Up Dark Horse Road

there is a bend where the mud-witch watches
  when you pass by
  you are in another land
  though it looks the same
  you know she has let you by
  her eyes are on your back
  you know she is made
  of moss and bark and skinny branches
  and that you are mostly water
  only skin separates you from her
  she is dry and you are wet
  because your voice is made of salt
  and you walk by in her land,
  notice, although you do not look,
  that the wind always picks up here.
  Yes it does.

If you were Keats or Shelley
or any of the male poets
it would have something to say to you,
something with words in it,
but the wind in the trees on Dark Horse Road
at that place beyond the mud-witch
has nothing to say to you at all.
You wish you could hear
because you know, metaphorically speaking,
the wind in the trees must be more

than that. That is the problem.
The wind remains as it is
and the sea too, rushing in and out,
trees full of light in the evening at nine
have no more to say than that.

The deer do not say more
down in the long grass.
We exchange eloquent glances
but no words and I a woman
supposed to be part of it all
at one at least. All the male poets
are good at this. They make the stones talk.

Once I heard a stone.
"Ouch!" I said, "you're made of fire."
"You better believe it honey,"
and I dropped it like a hot potato
the end of any conversation with stones
not that I don't like their warmth.
I lie down on a stone full of sun by the sea
and the sea is not a good place to start
a poem with all its coming and going.
That is the problem with these incessant things.
They hum. Regard the bees beside the marsh,

the green flashing humming bird
inside the foxglove along the gaudy edge,

the blue edge of a continent.

I know there is a yellow river the colour of mud
a swath of lawn the breadth of a hair
where I stand unable to speak.
That was always the problem.

Down Dark Horse Road

the children go
down on their bikes
Joanie in her white hat
pedaling, and all
the Mums and Dads go too,
to Russell's Reef for a swim
in the late afternoon
on a summer's day.

I sit at my desk
as others go down,
hold back always looking
out a window at the world,
bad parallel to the Lady
of Shalott. She only saw
reflections, turned around
and drowned. Didn't desire
just drown her? Where to put
the word — in a house, a forest,
a mountaintop? The blank space.

If I describe everything
around me and outside
my window if I describe
within and without I think
I would still be missing
removing myself to say

the white grasses seed white ripe
their tops bend gold-white

when I do not know
and a single glance can do
as much as the sharp blind
white grass whiting out the world.
There must be a way back.

I am able to tell them
where the milk is
how to find cinnamon buns
I bought this morning
at the store, that the butter
dish is on the counter.

At night when I lie on the tent platform
the stars sway back and forth.

There are stories of women who will not stop
crying. Where do they live?
On what street? No one can comfort
them. People would like to go
back into their houses.
She has become an irritant.
Who wants such a woman under their skin?
Who wants such a woman?

I have come to a place
where the white grass ripens where the stars
sway back and forth in the wind.

Continental Drift

I came here to look at an edge
for the first time,
a continent

a distance to come
to an island where the air hums.
In what story

does the woman cry unable to stop,
no longer pretending
to belong, something that wants
to come out

of the vast spreading away
of the sky of the day
the huge waves of green
a humming
no solid certain thing

give me something
that will not slip away
a cup a mug a glass of wine
a mango in its skin
I am as the same

the emptiness that leaps
beyond me to the blue land

across water

and there is a river
a pile of earth
there is a bridge
and a church and a woman
in a white dress in an alley

she's mad as a teacup mad as a wet hen
mad as mad her voice
sings into the chaotic red place
into the fall of the brain
a baroque pineapple convolution
between her legs
exotic as a dish of pistachios
the edge

of another body across
so much space
and the blue eating
away of distinctions I do not want
to dissolve the host that might bleed

I paint
my walls yellow to stop
stop in somewhere solid
I am a quiet woman.
I do not dance anymore
the sound of my own body

roaring how can this be?
How does the world
come in to such a quiet woman?

A stick in my hand the night
on each side.

Penelope's Windowboxes

I have come at a dangerous time.

the road north covered in leaves
it is the green road still wet
glittering after a rain
plant me down plant me green
among your green things
beside your bowl of oranges

She says I have slow feet and am always heading north,
turn into darkness, arms outstretched, dread the cold,
come out of the woods at dusk holding nothing.
I am always the same man hedging home.
A body alarmed by a bowl of oranges.
Too much sea. She says the petunias
never this purple, before *tantem ergo
sacramentum*, the evening unconsummated,
and afloat I dream of going north.
She sits beside a purple overflow.
I have come at a dangerous time.

the road north covered in leaves
it is the green road still wet
glittering after a rain
plant me down plant me green
among your green things
beside your bowl of oranges

strange the light seeping through that thick blue bowl

The ship groans stops dead the tree
in winter tied fast to the land,
nowhere to go.
The bones of her face small bones,
on the moss green floor of the earth bones.
"What ails you?" she asks.
From my mouth the dark night north.
I would be gone if not for you.

Sonata For G.

A moon that wavers like a room I try
to walk across evenings like this. You see
what happens? Lunch together
and then I lie in bed lubricious
suspicious at my age, and magnolia trees
wacky with buds — a pink gin fizz.

> (Noting gloves — always the flat, black
> fingers of one glove splayed wide,
> sodden on sidewalks. Good
> to have a focus: a glove
> randomly, a place called the end
> of the world out of order
> out of hand.)

If I was a wacky pink fizz tree
on alternate evenings I'd flirt
in the endless sun, in summer
dresses (pink) with an astronomer
who'd kiss me beneath the silvery
moon, alive aliveoh, but …

> (I watch you from the 6th floor of the library
> where Leonor Fini (see Surrealist, see Female,
> see Artist) and *Le Bout Du Monde* (see Painting)
> struggle (and you'll never understand, never)
> to represent subject gendered position and
> locations of female eroticism existing in fragments
> of systemic duplicity…)

I throw down my black glove

at your feet
        (you think it's a test)
and say the eventual end of the universe,
well, upsets me. I am a dizzy
damsel in distress. You give
me my hand and suggest
The End of Time
        (the book)
might cheer me up for a moment or two.
Shaken apart on a summer's afternoon
with three crows in a tree and a man
beside me at the end
of time like an arrow the hairs on his arm.

What To Do After A Miscarriage

1. Principal Vellum

Did anything happen?

That night in my mother's bed the blankets swept
off me:
Wake up! Wake up, dear!
She huge and all swift motion
tears the sheets off. Why is she afraid of the sheets?
What is in the bed? I shiver
in my pajamas; see something dark spreading.

I used to eat my mother's bed
gnawed the wooden spools
with sharp milk teeth
licked the straight scraped lines
made by my mouth

There! The new sheets shaken out. She sighs
and they fall into place. Something on me
wet did I wet the bed? Now she seizes me.
The black thing wiggles across the sheets.
Is it a snake? Off come my pajamas,
my mother a rushing force
like the wind through the trees

Everything's all right. Mummy's here.
Lifted. Carried.

I was in my mother's big wooden bed the night she handled a miscarriage.

The ultra-sound test: a deep sea sounding

to hear if there is still life
                    (a pear floating in a white space
                    a brace of pheasants in an equivalent
                                        of silence
                    a fetus against a dark ground)
still life inside of me

2. Recourse   What to do

taking the waters taking lunch
these are cures my mother knows
e.g. if you are insane she'll run you a hot bath,
after you have a miscarriage
she'll drive you down to the Arbutus Village
                                        Shopping Mall
hiss through the wet streets
                    (if the parking lot is crowded then
                                        everyone has
                    had a miscarriage today)

one-out-of-three-of-us ushered

through the automatic doors, past Safeway,
the rows of potted mums (muted bronzes) —
an even distribution of music everywhere
like salve applied to skin. A quiet place for lunch
my mother knows; all rose and gold,
mannequins reach out arms behind glass,
on ledges crouch trees in clay pots.
They mean no harm at the the edge of the woods
where signs point to a Realty World
so we must be here with pictures
of bungalows all in a row —
palliative perhaps. Take two with water.

What holds us together?

Band-Aids of colour wrap around walls
discrete as flesh: a virtue of inoffensiveness.

3. Coda   Lunch at the Arbutus Mall after a miscarriage
offers
croissants, cream cheese, Cappuccinos
        pale fluffy food and the flowery taste of air
        that reminds me of my aunt's top dresser drawer
        all her gloves and stitched hankies
        and tins of lavender candies dusted with powered
        sugar
        a mauve sweet nausea
        an excess of pastel prints on the wall
                (mine/my mother's/my aunt's?)

misty lily ponds, trees receding
chin-like to the edges of walled gardens
          (pallid exposures that reference a feminist
concern)
there there she pats my hand suggests dessert
she says

it's time to go
we retrace our steps through the trees,
past the wan mums, out the glass doors
back into the rain black now and cold.

4. Marginalia   A non-event is full of edges
margins of long illuminated letters,
coils of angels,
crowded with griffins
and a sun wheels round and round a giddy glittering
thing
while the earth stands still decorous as white linen.

The First Swimming Lesson

Coming out of Holden we stop for gas.
Back down the road on a morning
too cold to swim our niece stands undecided
on astro turf her shoulders sharp as the saran
wrapped wings on sale at the supermarket.
For the space of a morning
there are too many things out of place.

1) The deer should not be in the graveyard
   across from the gas station.
2) The children should not be blue-lipped
   in that glaucous one-eyed pool.
   The whistle blows
   they jump in
   water slops
   over the edge
   and the turf soaks up
   dark as a rat.
3) The chain link fence between the highway
   and where the children swim
   is no guarantee and spiders
   spin their webs across the holes.
4) Finally, the deer is not dead.

   Here are things that rise and fall :
   i)   the breath
   ii) the heart

iii) the sun

iv) inflections

v) infections

and the black unruled diamond

spare hoofs of the deer

With the car windows sealed as shut as the silence of heaven

    — a feathered thing shot dead — I hope

    (I am after all in Emily's land)

    for

    a stone basin

    a fountain of water to tread

    an encircling nascency of stars

    to annunciate

    the proper name

    of this girl this deer this place

    swimming.

Locating Lazarus .

Here. In a big pause askance
at the nettles that thrive on my septic field, and evening
touching the wavering sky
and sea with sudden light I wonder

about Lazarus; idle around him. He is still
there. There are the usual questions:

> where was he for three days
> how could anyone look him in the eye again
> was he glad to touch things or did they slide

from his fingers—people and skin, bowls, animals, a comb,
thread. It is hard to know.

> was he regarded as a ghost what
> protected him when unwrapped

Think Lazarus absently (mostly crazy to get away with you in August)

— the photo I keep: a group of astronomers in Hawaii. They stand
   on their shadows   at 5:30 already long
   flowers around their necks they are all smiling

because it is a special occasion and they are all having their pictures
                     taken at dusk
(you bit me gently on my right shoulder I said kiss me longer
  you did)

Lazarus absently in terms of how wrapped
in linen and dead he might after —
to the end of his days could not recall the stone above his eyes
salt grit there at the door of his house
stood there alone upon a peak in Darien waiting
the ways to his own door come upon a volume of stone

where you are

this time around me threads nouns dropped
verbs move by glacially adversely
adverbially they went to seed packaged wanly
after the apocalyptic
proportions of the golden mean
biblical and meaningful meaning this hesitancy

if you sat across from me as you have
I would say like the song here I am
in your silence you try to think this and work hard

so that there is no time really you are busy
I too
have
my work

the stars perverse proportions inverse a terse voice voce voce
veni
went

Lazarus blinking the butterflies
blinking in the heat of a moment dark
at the centre of a plum stone

Spider Notes

Spiders seize onto anything; a stone
a piece of bone, the back of a chair,
or the porch. Foxgloves. The house itself.

If I put down my cup
a spider
will start
to thread it
to the green bottle
on the deck railing.
Soon

there is nothing I can pick up
that is not a piece of something else

If I drop the cup
the house will break.
I hate being so careful
so I take off my gold wedding band,
place it on the windowsill
where it can grow into the waterglass
and catch flies.
Snap!
Like that.

Acknowledgements

Poems from this collection have appeared in *Event* (New Westminster), and *The Fiddlehead* (Fredericton).

I would like to give special thanks to Roger Semmens who noticed, and to George McWhirter who brought the gift of his remarkably shrewd and always magical perception to this manuscript.

I am grateful to Jerry Newman, Kate Braid, Luanne Armstrong, Ramona Dearing, Lorraine Weir, Stephanie Bolster, Tammy Armstrong, Linda Bailey, Jennifer Mitton, Doug Guildford, Karon Graham, Terry Power, and, of course, my dear family, for their belief in me.

Thanks also to the University of British Columbia's Department of Creative Writing and the Graduate Fellowship Fund.

Above all, to Charles Reif for his love and support in difficult times, I give my heartfelt thanks.